Twenty

Twenty
Stella Benson

MINT EDITIONS

Twenty was first published in 1918.

This edition published by Mint Editions 2021.

ISBN 9781513291185 | E-ISBN 9781513294032

Published by Mint Editions®

**MINT
EDITIONS**

minteditionbooks.com

Publishing Director: Jennifer Newens
Design & Production: Rachel Lopez Metzger
Project Manager: Micaela Clark
Typesetting: Westchester Publishing Services

Contents

Preface

Almost all the verses in this book have appeared before, the majority of them included in two books, *I Pose* and *This is the End*. Messrs. Macmillan, who published these, have been kind in raising no objection to re-publication. I have also to thank the Editors of the *Athenaeum*, *Everyman*, and the *Pall Mall Gazette* for allowing me to reprint verses.

The title of the book has no reference to the writer's age.

S.B.

Christmas, 1917

A key no thief can steal, no time can rust;
A faery door, adventurous and golden;
A palace, perfect to our eyes—Ah must
Our eyes be holden?

Has the past died before this present sin?
Has this most cruel age already stonèd
To martyrdom that magic Day, within
Those halls, enthronèd?

No. Through the dancing of the young spring rain,
Through the faint summer, and the autumn's burning,
Our still immortal Day has heard again
Our steps returning.

The Secret Day

My yesterday has gone, has gone and left me tired,
And now tomorrow comes and beats upon the door;
So I have built Today, the day that I desired,
Lest joy come not again, lest peace return no more,
Lest comfort come no more.

So I have built Today, a proud and perfect day,
And I have built the towers of cliffs upon the sands;
The foxgloves and the gorse I planted on my way;
The thyme, the velvet thyme, grew up beneath my hands,
Grew pink beneath my hands.

So I have built Today, more precious than a dream;
And I have painted peace upon the sky above;
And I have made immense and misty seas, that seem
More kind to me than life, more fair to me than love—
More beautiful than love.

And I have built a house—a house upon the brink
Of high and twisted cliffs; the sea's low singing fills it;
And there my Secret Friend abides, and there I think
I'll hide my heart away before tomorrow kills it—
A cold tomorrow kills it.

Yes, I have built Today, a wall against Tomorrow,
So let Tomorrow knock—I shall not be afraid,
For none shall give me death, and none shall give me sorrow,
And none shall spoil this darling day that I have made.
No storm shall stir my sea. No night but mine shall shade
This day that I have made.

Song

There is the track my feet have worn
By which my fate may find me:
From that dim place where I was born
Those footprints run behind me.
Uncertain was the trail I left,
For—oh, the way was stormy;
But now this splendid sea has cleft
My journey from before me.

Three things the sea shall never end,
Three things shall mock its power:
My singing soul, my Secret Friend,
And this, my perfect hour.
And you shall seek me till you reach
The tangled tide advancing,
And you shall find upon the beach
The traces of my dancing,
And in the air the happy speech
Of Secret Friends romancing.

The Orchard

I will repent me of my ways;
I will come here and bury
Five thousand odd superfluous days
Beneath a flow'ring cherry.

Between a pear and a cherry tree
My temple I will enter—
My place, where even I may be
The altar and the centre.

One altar to a thousand aisles,
A hundred thousand arches. . .
The loud lamb-choir about me files,
The bleating bishop marches,

The congregation kneels and nods,
The bishop leads its praises,
So I'll pray too, to their dim gods
Whose feet are decked with daisies:

> *Ah, let me not grow old. Ah, let*
> *Me not grow old, and falter*
> *In my delusion, or forget*
> *My heart was once an altar.*
> *Let me still think myself a star*
> *With these my rays about me;*
> *Pretend these green perspectives are*
> *All purposeless without me.*
>
> *Ah, bid the sun stand still. Ah, bid*
> *The coming night retire,*
> *And all the good I ever did*
> *Shall feed your altar fire;*
> *The hour shall stand and sing your praise,*
> *The minute shall adore you,*

And my ten thousand unborn days
I'll sacrifice before you.

Gods of great joy, and little grief,
See—I will wear as token
A pear leaf and a cherry leaf
Until this pledge be broken. . .

Between a pear and a cherry tree
A cold hand touched my shoulder—
Ah, my false gods have forsaken me,
I am a minute older.

Thanks to My World for the Loan of a Fair Day

That day you wrought for me
Shone, and was ended.
Perfect your thought for me,
Whom you befriended.
Such joy was new to me—
New, and most splendid,
More than was due to me.
More than was due to me.

Though I do wrong to you,
Having no power,
Singing no song to you,
Bringing no flower,
Yet does my youth again
Thrill, for the hour
Cometh in truth again.
Cometh in truth again.

I shall possess today
All I have wanted,
All I lacked yesterday
Now shall be granted.
No longer dumb to you,
Changed and enchanted,
Singing I'll come to you.
Singing I'll come to you.

I will amass for you
Very great treasure.
Swift years shall pass for you
Dancing for pleasure.
Time shall be slave to me,
Giving—full measure—
All that you gave to me.
All that you gave to me.

Song

If I have dared to surrender some imitation of splendour,
Something I knew that was tender, something I loved that was brave,
If in my singing I showed songs that I heard on my road,
Were they not debts that I owed, rather than gifts that I gave?

If certain hours on their climb up the long ladder of time
Turned my confusion to rhyme, drove me to dare an attempt,
If by fair chance I might seem sometimes abreast of my theme,
Was I translating a dream? Was it a dream that you dreamt?

High and miraculous skies bless and astonish my eyes;
All my dead secrets arise, all my dead stories come true.
Here is the Gate to the Sea. Once you unlocked it for me;
Now, since you gave me the key, shall I unlock it for you?

WORDS

Oh words, oh words, and shall you rule
The world? What is it but the tongue
That doth proclaim a man a fool,
So that his best songs go unsung,
So that his dreams are sent to school
And all die young.

There pass the trav'lling dreams, and these
My soul adores—my words condemn—
Oh, I would fall upon my knees
To kiss their golden garments' hem,
Yet words do lie in wait to seize
And murder them.

Tonight the swinging stars shall plumb
The silence of the sky. And herds
Of plumèd winds like huntsmen come
To hunt with dreams the restless birds.
Tonight the moon shall strike you dumb,
Oh words, oh words. . .

STELLA BENSON

Redneck's Song

These thirty years
Old men have filled my ears
With middle-aged ideas
That never have been young,
They made me wise.
I learnt to whitewash lies.
I learnt to shut my eyes,
And hold my tongue.

Damned Philistine.
And was it then so fine
To learn to draw the line.
(Is there a line to draw?)
And must I then
For threescore years and ten
Worship the laws of men
Who worshipped law?

Those laws are dust
Today, and yet I must
Be faithful still, and trust
In what dead men did prove.
Magic may kill
Their wisdom and their will,
Yet I must follow still
Their path. . . my groove. . .

To the Unborn

Oh, bend your eyes, nor send your glance about.
Oh, watch your feet, nor stray beyond the kerb.
Oh, bind your heart lest it find secrets out.
For thus no punishment
Of magic shall disturb
Your very great content.

Oh, shut your lips to words that are forbidden.
Oh, throw away your sword, nor think to fight.
Seek not the best, the best is better hidden.
Thus need you have no fear,
No terrible delight
Shall cross your path, my dear.

Call no man foe, but never love a stranger.
Build up no plan, nor any star pursue.
Go forth with crowds; in loneliness is danger.
Thus nothing God can send,
And nothing God can do
Shall pierce your peace, my friend.

The Newer Zion

When I achieve the chestnut joke of dying,
When I slip through that Gate at Kensal Green,
Shall I go spoil the fantasy by prying
Behind the staging of this darling scene?

Shall I—a cast-off puppet—seek to study
The Showman who manipulates the strings,
The Hand that paints the western drop-scene ruddy,
The prosy truths of all these faery things?

Shall I—self-conscious by a glassy ocean—
Stammer strange songs amid an alien host?
Or shall I not, refusing such promotion,
Bequeath to London my contented ghost?

I will come back to my Eternal City;
Her fogs once more my countenance shall dim;
I will enliven your austere committee
With gossip gleaned among the cherubim.

By day I'll tread again the sounding mazes,
By night I'll track the moths about the Park;
My feet shall fall among the dusky daisies,
Nor break nor bruise a petal in the dark.

I will repeat old inexpensive orgies;
Drink nectar at the bun-shop in Shoreditch,
Or call for Nut-Ambrosia at St. George's,
And with a ghost-tip make the waitress rich.

My soundless feet shall fly among the runners
Through the red thunders of a Zeppelin raid,
My still voice cheer the Anti-Aircraft gunners,
The fires shall glare—but I shall cast no shade.

And if a Shadow, wading in the torrent
Of high excitement, snatch me from the riot—
(Fool that he is)—and fumble with his warrant,
And hail a hearse, and beg me to "Go quiet,"

Mocking I'll go, and he shall be postillion,
Until we reach the Keeper of the Door:
"H'm. . . Benson. . . Stella. . . militant civilian. . .
There's some mistake, we've had this soul before. . ."

*   *   *   *   *   *

Ah, none shall keep my soul from this its Zion;
Lost in the spaces I shall hear and bless
The splendid voice of London, like a lion
Calling its lover in the wilderness.

STELLA BENSON

Two Women Sing

First Woman

Oh woman—woman—woman,—
Shall I to woman be a friend?
I deal with man, and when I can
Reclaim with interest all I lend.
Who but a witless gambler plays
For farthing stakes these golden days?
No, woman—woman—woman—
Must only play the game that pays.

Second Woman

Oh woman—woman—woman,—
Tomorrow woman shall awake.
She shall arise, and realise
The goodly value of her stake.
And she shall lend her loan, and claim
Her rightful interest on the same.
So woman—woman—woman—
Shall learn at last the paying game.

The Woman Alone

My eyes are girt with outer mists;
My ears sing shrill, and this I bless;
My finger-nails do bite my fists
In ecstasy of loneliness.
This I intend, and this I want,
That—passing—you may only mark
A dumb soul with its confidant
Entombed together in the dark.

The hoarse church-bells of London ring;
The hoarser horns of London croak;
The poor brown lives of London cling
About the poor brown streets like smoke;
The deep air stands above my roof
Like water, to the floating stars.
My Friend and I—we sit aloof,—
We sit and smile, and bind our scars.

For you may wound and you may kill—
It's such a little thing to die—
Your cruel God may work his will,
We do not care, my Friend and I.
Though, at the gate of Paradise,
Peter the Saint withhold his keys,
My Friend and I—we have no eyes
For Heav'n or Hell—or dreams like these. . .

The Inevitable

There is a sword, a fatal blade,
Unthwarted, subtle as the air,
And I could meet it unafraid
If I might only meet it fair.
Yet how I wonder why the Smith
Who wrought that steel of subtle grain
Should also be contented with
So blunt and mean a thing as pain.

The stars and fire-flies dance in rings.
The fire-flies set my heart alight,
Like fingers, writing magic things
In flame, upon the wall of night.
There is high meaning in the skies—
(The stars and fire-flies—high and low—)
And all the spangled world is wise
With knowledge that I almost know.

Tomorrow I will don my cloak
Of opal-grey, and I will stand
Where the palm-shadows stride like smoke
Across the dazzle of the sand.
Tomorrow I will throw this blind
Blind whiteness from my soul away,
And pluck this blackness from my mind,
And only leave the medium—grey.

Tomorrow I will cry for gains
Upon the blue and brazen sky.
The precious venom in my veins
Tomorrow will be parched and dry.
Tomorrow it shall be my goal
To throw myself away from me,
To lose the outline of my soul
Against the greyness of the sea.

THE DOG TUPMAN

Oh little friend of half my days,
My little friend, who followed me
Along those crooked sullen ways
That only you had eyes to see.

You felt the same. You understood
You too, defensive and morose,
Encloaked your secret puppyhood—
Your secret heart—and hid them close.

For I alone have seen you serve,
Disciple of those early springs,
With ears awry and tail a-curve
You lost yourself in puppy things.

And you saw me. You bore in mind
The clean and sunny things I felt
When, throwing hate along the wind,
I flashed the lantern at my belt.

The moment passed, and we returned
To barren words and old cold truth,
Yet in our hearts our lanterns burned,
We two had seen each other's youth.

When filthy pain did wrap me round
Your upright ears I always saw,
And on my outflung hand I found
The blessing of your horny paw;

And yet—oh impotence of men—
My paw, more soft but not more wise,
Old friend, was lacking to you when
You looked your crisis in the eyes. . .

You shared my youth, oh faithful friend,
You let me share your puppyhood;
So, if I failed you in the end,
My friend, my friend, you understood.

Saint Bride

About your brow a starry wreath,
About your feet a wilderness,
Where young hot hopes grow cold beneath
The tangled bondage of the press.
Set like a saint within a niche—
A strait and narrow niche—you hide,
And weave a veil about you, which
Can turn our steel, Saint Bride, Saint Bride.

The eyes of coarse and pond'rous man
Are sceptic and satirical.
"What, little saint, and still you scan
Old heaven for that miracle?"
Oh heart deceived, yet harmèd not,
Child-widow of a truth that died,
Bearer in mind of things forgot,
Bride of a dream, Saint Bride, Saint Bride.

About you and about you thunders
The wise young public on its 'bus,
Exploding all your faery blunders,
Explaining neatly—*"Thus and thus*
Hath science banished heaven now,
And see—your Groom is crucified—"
On heaven's breast you lean your brow
And laugh, and love—Saint Bride, Saint Bride.

The Slave of God

The finest fruit God ever made
Hangs from the Tree of Heaven blue.
It hangs above the steel sea blade
That cuts the world's great globe in two.

The keenest eye that ever saw
Stares out of Heaven into mine,
Spins out my heart, and seems to draw
My soul's elastic very fine.

The greatest beacon ever fired
Stands up on Heaven's Hill to show
The limit of the thing desired,
Beyond which man may never go.

    *   *   *   *   *   *

At midnight, when the night did dance
Along the hours that led to morning,
I saw a little boat advance
Towards the great moon's beacon warning.

(The moon, God's Slave, who lights her torch,
Lest men should slip between the bars,
And run aground on Heav'n, and scorch
To death upon a bank of stars.)

The little boat, on leaning keel,
Sang up the mountains of the sea,
Bearing a man who hoped to steal
God's Slave from out eternity.

"My love, I see you through my tears.
No pity in your face I see.
I have sailed far across the years:
Stretch out, stretch out your arms to me.

"My love, I have an island seen,
So shadowed, God's most piercing star
Shall never see where we have been,
Shall never whisper where we are.

"There we will wander, you and I,
Down guilty and delightful ways,
While palm-trees plait their fingers high
Against your God's enormous gaze.

"For oh—the joy of two and two
Your Paradise shall never see,
The ecstasy of me and you,
The white delight of you and me.

"I know the penalty—the clutch
Of God's great rocks upon my keel.
Drowned in the ocean of Too Much—
So ends your thief—yet let me steal. . ."

The Slave of God she froze her face,
The Slave of God she paid no heed,
And, thund'ring down high Heaven's space,
Loud angels mocked the sailor's greed.

The diamond sun arose, and tossed
A billion gems across the sea.
"The Slave of God is lost, is lost,
The Slave of God is lost to me. . ."

He grounded on the common beach,
He trod the little towns of men,
And God removèd from his reach
The cup of Heaven's passion then,
And gave him vulgar love and speech,
And gave him threescore years and ten.

TRUE PROMISES

You promised War and Thunder and Romance.
You promised true, but we were very blind
And very young, and in our ignorance
We never called to mind
That truth is seldom kind.

You promised love, immortal as a star.
You promised true, yet how the truth can lie!
For now we grope for hands where no hands are,
And, deathless, still we cry,
Nor hope for a reply.

You promised harvest and a perfect yield.
You promised true, for on the harvest morn,
Behold a reaper strode across the field,
And man of woman born
Was gathered in as corn.

You promised honour and ordeal by flame.
You promised true. In joy we trembled lest
We should be found unworthy when it came;
But—oh—we never guessed
The fury of the test!

You promised friends and songs and festivals.
You promised true. Our friends, who still are young,
Assemble for their feasting in those halls
Where speaks no human tongue.
And thus our songs are sung.

The Cornishman

At sunset, when the high sea span
About the rocks a web of foam,
I saw the ghost of a Cornishman
Come home.
I saw the ghost of a Cornishman
Run from the weariness of war,
I heard him laughing as he ran
Across his unforgotten shore.
The great cliff, gilded by the west,
Received him as an honoured guest.
The green sea, shining in the bay,
Did drown his dreadful yesterday.

Come home, come home, you million ghosts,
The honest years shall make amends,
The sun and moon shall be your hosts,
The everlasting hills your friends.
And some shall seek their mothers' faces,
And some shall run to trysting places,
And some to towns, and others yet
Shall find great forests in their debt.
    Oh, I would siege the golden coasts
    Of space, and climb high heaven's dome,
    So I might see those million ghosts
    Come home.

Five Smooth Stones

It was young David, lord of sheep and cattle,
Pursued his fate, the April fields among,
Singing a song of solitary battle,
A loud mad song, for he was very young.

Vivid the air—and something more than vivid,—
Tall clouds were in the sky—and something more,—
The light horizon of the spring was livid
With a steel smile that showed the teeth of war.

It was young David mocked the Philistine.
It was young David laughed beside the river.
There came his mother—his and yours and mine—
With five smooth stones, and dropped them in his quiver.

You never saw so green-and-gold a fairy.
You never saw such very April eyes.
She sang him sorrow's song to make him wary,
She gave him five smooth stones to make him wise.

The first stone is love, and that shall fail you.
The second stone is hate, and that shall fail you.
The third stone is knowledge, and that shall fail you.
The fourth stone is prayer, and that shall fail you.
The fifth stone shall not fail you.

For what is love, O lovers of my tribe?
And what is love, O women of my day?
Love is a farthing piece, a bloody bribe
Pressed in the palm of God—and thrown away.

And what is hate, O fierce and unforgiving?
And what shall hate achieve, when all is said?
A silly joke that cannot reach the living,
A spitting in the faces of the dead.

And what is knowledge, O young men who tasted
The reddest fruit on that forbidden tree?
Knowledge is but a painful effort wasted,
A bitter drowning in a bitter sea.

And what is prayer, O waiters for the answer?
And what is prayer, O seekers of the cause?
Prayer is the weary soul of Herod's dancer,
Dancing before blind kings without applause.

The fifth stone is a magic stone, my David,
Made up of fear and failure, lies and loss.
Its heart is lead, and on its face is gravèd
A crookèd cross, my son, a crookèd cross.

It has no dignity to lend it value;
No purity—alas, it bears a stain.
You shall not give it gratitude, nor shall you
Recall it all your days, except with pain.

Oh, bless your blindness, glory in your groping!
Mock at your betters with an upward chin!
And when the moment has gone by for hoping,
Sling your fifth stone, O son of mine, and win.

Grief do I give you, grief and dreadful laughter;
Sackcloth for banner, ashes in your wine.
Go forth, go forth, nor ask me what comes after;
The fifth stone shall not fail you, son of mine.

GO FORTH, GO FORTH, AND SLAY THE PHILISTINE.

New Year, 1918

A song I never heard
I must rehearse,
Counting each hour a word,
Counting each day a verse.
Not of my proper choice
Raise I my voice,
While others—fierce and strong—
Raise theirs to drown my song.

Must I then sing aloud,
Faint as a bird,
And, like a bird, be proud
To sing—to sing unheard?
Weary and very weak,
Shall I then seek
A hearing, idiot-wise,
From the unhearing skies?

Drowning my whispered dreams,
Great voices cry.
They sing their songs, it seems,
With better heart than I.
Hush—I can hear Death sing—
"Here is my sting."
And the Grave echo—*"See,
Here is my victory"*

Tonight the heavens bend
A little nearer.
The singer is my friend,
And I—at last—the hearer.
No more to sing alone
A song unknown,—
Hush—very tense and thin,
The dawn-like notes begin.

A Note About the Author

Stella Benson (1892–1933) was an English feminist poet, travel writer, and novelist. Born into a wealthy Shropshire family, Benson was the niece of bestselling novelist Mary Cholmondeley. Educated from a young age, she lived in London, Germany, and Switzerland in her youth, which was marked by her parents' acrimonious separation. As a young woman in London, she became active in the women's suffrage movement, which informed her novels *This Is the End* (1917) and *Living Alone* (1919). In 1918, Benson traveled to the United States, settling in Berkley for a year and joining the local Bohemian community. In 1920, she met her husband in China and began focusing on travel writing with such essay collections and memoirs as *The Little World* (1925) and *World Within Worlds* (1928). Benson, whose work was admired by Virginia Woolf, continued publishing novels, stories, and poems until her death from pneumonia in the Vietnamese province of Tonkin.

A Note from the Publisher

Spanning many genres, from non-fiction essays to literature classics to children's books and lyric poetry, Mint Edition books showcase the master works of our time in a modern new package. The text is freshly typeset, is clean and easy to read, and features a new note about the author in each volume. Many books also include exclusive new introductory material. Every book boasts a striking new cover, which makes it as appropriate for collecting as it is for gift giving. Mint Edition books are only printed when a reader orders them, so natural resources are not wasted. We're proud that our books are never manufactured in excess and exist only in the exact quantity they need to be read and enjoyed.

bookfinity™

Discover more of your favorite classics with Bookfinity™.

- Track your reading with custom book lists.
- Get great book recommendations for your personalized Reader Type.
- Add reviews for your favorite books.
- AND MUCH MORE!

Visit **bookfinity.com** and take the fun Reader Type quiz to get started.

Enjoy our classic and modern companion pairings!

Classic & Modern

www.ingramcontent.com/pod-product-compliance
Lightning Source LLC
Chambersburg PA
CBHW020446030426
42337CB00014B/1416